Why Inventions Fail to Sell

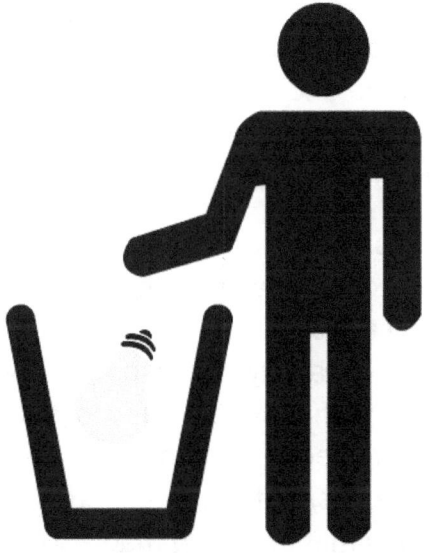

And How to Go From Ideas to Profits Inside 30 Days

by Rob Gramer

Go to www.inventionprep.com to learn how to start profiting off your idea in the next 30 days.

Inside:

Go to www.inventionprep.com to learn how to start profiting off your idea in the next 30 days.

25 How to sell products to the golf market (and how this simple example can tell you if you have a "winner" or not in any other market)

26 How to discover the "mental barriers" that prevent people from buying your product

31 For even the simplest of ideas you will spend - at least - THOUSANDS of dollars on design and engineering. The simple step that 99 out of 100 inventors skip that will a) help you turn a profit in the first 30 days WITHOUT a finished product...b)give you enough money to create a prototype and end product without you having to dig into savings...and c) find investors to fund your idea (which you probably won't even need after taking this simple step)

33 How much are you willing to spend on your idea? A simple example of how a $250,000 investment was reduced to $2.

34 3 weeks, or a year and a half? Same product. Same market. How to drastically shortcut getting your idea to market.

36 The sneaky trick advertising reps play to get you to spent THOUSANDS more on advertising space than you need (plus, how to save an ADDITIONAL 10-50% on any ad you buy)

39 The quickest way to sabotage sales of your invention

Go to www.inventionprep.com to learn how to
start profiting off your idea in the next 30 days.

Introduction

Most inventions fail to sell for one simple reason.

This short book tells you why.

It is the transcript of an interview with one of the world's top experts on why people buy what they buy.

Also known as market research.

And because of his expertise on finding out what a market (a group of people with a common interest) wants...what they are willing to pay...and the behaviors behind how they buy...he has a unique method of going from idea to profitability inside of 30 days.

This is NOT common...

Most inventors do NOT see a profit until months or years after having that idea (if they don't go broke first).

The technique in this book shortcuts that process.

And it allows you to skip a TON of the unnecessary steps most inventors think they must go through.

This book won't make you a million dollars.

But, it can save you from wasting thousands - perhaps HUNDREDS of thousands of dollars - and months (or years) of your life on an idea that won't sell.

Plus - if you do have a good idea - it will help you monetize that idea a lot sooner.

And, it can help you do both in a way that is fun, fast, and effective.

If after reading this interview you want to find out more about this expert, visit his website at www.dobermandan.com.

Rob Gramer: Thanks for being on the interview today, Dan. We've known each other for a while, but how about you let the listeners know where you are coming from.

Doberman Dan: Ok. Be glad to.

I kind of stumbled into entrepreneurship and marketing. Not much life planning plus career planning on my part.

I stumbled into what was my first real job when I was going to a community college. I had some friends talk to me in taking the Civil Service test for police officers in the city of Dayton, Ohio and never thought that I would actually make it through the selection process due to some poor choices when I was in high school (mainly involving marijuana, smoked a lot of weed in high school.)

But anyways, I became a police officer. And after a few years I realized that I wanted to make more money and I wanted the freedom and the lifestyle of an entrepreneur and that led to various failed ventures for nine years straight until finally discovering what is called direct response marketing.

8

Rob Gramer: And what is that?

Doberman Dan: It's a certain type of marketing, as opposed to image advertising.

Image advertising is like the good year blimp. You fly that thing during a football game with the mere hope that people who've seen them, when it's time buy tires will think of Goodyear.

Direct response advertising is different. It targets the market very tightly and actually asks for an order like a salesman would.

So I discovered direct response marketing and got involved in it and that turned everything around. All of a sudden, my business, I was able to start numerous successful businesses. Then I sold my last business a couple of years ago and now I am doing marketing consulting and copywriting which is writing the advertising for various companies. So that's it in a nutshell.

Rob Gramer: Got it. And for the inventors who are listening to this, realize that once you've got your product, you now have to somehow

Go to www.inventionprep.com to learn how to start profiting off your idea in the next 30 days.

advertise it to the people that are going to buy it from you.

So image advertising, like splattering my advertising message across the Goodyear blimp, that's going to cost me quite a bit of money.

Let's talk about that really quick, the investment side of this.

How much is it's going to cost to get something up and running if I was going to run, you know, Goodyear blimp ads versus what you would do in direct response marketing?

Doberman Dan: Well, one of the benefits of direct response marketing is it is highly accountable.

In other words you will know to the penny your return on investment or any other factors in the process that you are measuring

For example, you invest a thousand dollars and you will know to the penny, how much money that brought in.

Did it bring back in your original thousand dollars and nothing more? Did it bring back positive ROI of 10%? And that's something you can't nail down at all with image advertising.

If you want to see what image advertising is, grab any U.S.A today or any major circulation magazine and look at the big fortune 500 companies.

A good example of the stupidest ads are car ads.

When you look at the ad, you don't even know they are trying to advertise cars. It will be some big picture, maybe a desert scene, and will have all of three words on it, like: freedom, thrill, excitement, and way down the bottom in tiny letters Nissan or something like that.

You can spend hundreds of thousands of dollars, millions of dollars and still not have any idea if your advertising is effective or not.

Rob Gramer: But with direct advertising, you'll know?

Doberman Dan: To give you a frame of reference...

My first successful business was in the bodybuilding market. I started that with a small ad in one of the

11

bodybuilding magazines that I only paid $200 for.

And I got l five times ROI from that $200.

Rob Gramer: Five times ROI? So you made $1000 from that one ad?

Doberman Dan: Yes. So I was able to started on a shoestring budget. Just to get proof of concept.

Once I saw that worked and saw what the numbers were, it was pretty dependable and predictable that as I scaled up and rolled out in more medium - which was at the time was more magazines and direct mail - I could pretty much approximate that I would get the same return on investment.

So lot less risk and a lot of times it really, definitely compared to image advertising, things can be tested on a shoestring budget.

Rob Gramer: So - if I am an inventor - and let's say I have invented a new baseball bat...

...I could go in a baseball magazine, maybe not like ESPN but say like a baseball news quarterly and possibly

12

buy some ad space in there. And then in that ad I could write, "hey listen I have got this new baseball bat, you can contact me, my name is John. I live on 123 Main Street, etc., just send a check of 50 bucks and I will send you this baseball bat.

That's really basic, but that's essentially what you are saying?

Doberman Dan: Yeah, exactly.

You just need to prove that there is a demand for this. And yeah ESPN magazine or whatever, may have their ad rates are just, you know prohibitively expensive. But let's say there's a smaller magazine that caters to that niche, has a smaller circulation.

You can check out what they call their media kit which gives you the prices they want to get for certain size of ads in the magazine.

By the way that doesn't mean that's what you have to pay. I have always been able to negotiate those cheaper.

Yeah you can put a small ad in there just as a test and it literally may only cost you a couple hundreds bucks to do that.

13

Go to www.inventionprep.com to learn how to start profiting off your idea in the next 30 days.

Rob Gramer: So how would somebody get a media kit?

Let's say they have found gone down to Barnes and Noble and looked at all the magazines they have in there on the subject matter at hand.

How would they go about requesting a media kit to get those prices for ad space?

Doberman Dan: You can do it the old fashioned way like I had to do it when I first started because the internet was not even available to us civilians back then.

Just look in the front of the magazine. There's usually a list of departments, always have advertising listed with the phone number.

You just call them up and say send me your media kit. They may ask you a few questions, just tell them, it's for a new business that I am testing.

But also if you look up the magazine's website online, nowadays many if not most of them, you can either request the media kit online or they just put the whole media kit online that you can download as a pdf, just look near the

14

bottom. You will find the link which says something like advertise with us or something like that.

Rob Gramer: Got it, okay.

And to clarify, this is something called direct response marketing.

A lot of the inventors that I have talked to, their dream is to get the product on a store shelf so when somebody walks into a store and they see and they buy it.

Whereas what you are talking about is kind of getting right in front of these people.

They pick up a magazine, they read it, they say ok, that's something interesting I might want to buy.

And I know the big reason why you like this is what you have just said. It's much cheaper to test, you know, for a couple of hundred dollars versus thousands and thousands (which is what it would cost you to get in a retail location).

With that in mind, if, let's say I am your average inventor and I've just made a product. What would be your

15

advice to me? What would you say to me? What would you say to me to put my product in front of these people? What are the, 2,3,4,5 steps that I have to do from there?

Doberman Dan: Good question. To be totally transparent I should probably tell you that I have never started a business that way.

And based on my 20 years as a serial entrepreneur, I have always looked for a demand first.

I have looked for the market and the market demand first before ever developing a product because the way I do it, when I do market research first, the research tells me what kind of product to develop.

But I realized that inventors don't have that kind of marketing experience. So in almost every case, they come up with the idea first and come up with the product first, then they figure out who to sell this to.

It's completely backward in my opinion and you can lose years of your life and millions of dollars doing it that way.

So I am going to help people avoid that pain and suffering. Because it really sucks to lose years of your life and hundreds of thousands or millions of dollars and just the disappointment that goes along with that.

Worse is the brother in law laughing at you the entire time too...telling you, "I told you so".

We definitely want to help people avoid that.

Rob Gramer: So just to make sure everybody understands what Dan just said. He said that he is not inventing a product and then looking for somebody to sell it to.

He is going to look for people who are actively handing over money for something or want something and then he is going to make that something to sell them.

Is that correct?

Doberman Dan: It really is that simple. I have resources, if you want me to talk about them in depth I will but I'll just cover them briefly now.

I have resources that will tell me exactly, you know, let's just pick a market, say medical. So I can look up using my research tool, I can look up things in the medical market or doctors and find out what they are buying, what price points they are buying at, how many are buying, how many are buying monthly, how many have bought over the past six months, twelve months, twenty four months, five year maybe and it's that simple.

Once I find out what they are already buying, they are voting with their wallet, no focus groups, no surveys needed.

I mean I don't care what people say in a survey or focus group because people lie.

I never listen to what's coming out of their mouth, I just watch their actions. And the most important action is people voting with their wallet, with their money.

So once I find out what they are buying, it's pretty much a slam dunk to sell them more of the same or sell them something related that supports what they are already buying.

Somebody buying a high priced engineering software (Rob, you are an engineer) is a darn good candidate for a DVD series showing them how to use it or showing them shortcuts or tips and tricks.

That's just an example.

Now somebody comes to me backwards and they don't know this marketing stuff and they have done it backwards, come up with the product first, the first question I ask is who is it for?

Who is your target market?

So, then we have to do my research method at that point and we may discover one or two things that their idea was a good one and we can show that people(we can first of all find the market) are already buying something similar or that what support products that people are buying.

Or we might confirm that, that is a bad idea and nobody is going to buy it.

We might even find several other people that tried to sell it and if fall on flat on the face.

Either way it's good news, one we either save them from the brother in law making fun of them stuff and saving lots of money...

...or two, we've confirmed by seeing that people are voting for that idea with their wallets, then it is a good idea.

Rob Gramer: Yeah. And I think that's a very interesting point because you don't want to be that guy who invented underwater toilet paper.

It may be a great idea but how many people are hitting the john underneath the water?

So what you are really talking about here is a difference between a great idea and the difference between a great idea that has a built in desire that people want to buy it and people are willing to handover money for it?

Doberman Dan: That's exactly right. And it's best to do this as early as possible - especially if you don't have $100,000 or more to blow through testing the idea out - in the process before much time, effort and money is invested in the idea.

Go to www.inventionprep.com to learn how to start profiting off your idea in the next 30 days.

It's best to get an experienced marketing person involved in the beginning because you know they could be worth your weight in gold either by saving you all that time and money on something that's for sure to flop or confirming that you've got a, as I like to call them, a home run on your hands.

Rob Gramer: Right, because I know you've seen this and I have seen this countless times too...as soon as you get an idea, it's like a seed.

And then you start putting more time, money and emotion to it and then it grows.

And if it's an idea that will never sell, some people get married to that and then you know, months go by and years go by, and they end up throwing good money after bad.

And they are so convinced that it's such a good idea and the more and more time, more and more energy and more and more money into it, the more they get married to it.

And it's just ends up being something that takes on a life of its own and takes up all their time, and money, and

21

prevents them from moving onto the true goal...which is making more money from their ideas rather than investing and dumping money into their ideas.

Doberman Dan: Exactly, there's even a psychological term for that which I ran across few weeks back and I can't remember.

But it turns normally intelligent, rational, logical people into complete idiots.

Because the numbers which show any logical person that this is - as my marketing mentor used to say ATP (Abandon this product) - I mean any person who could look at it logically will think, I have got to abandon this as soon as possible.

But once they get passed a certain point and have emotional energy or money and time invested in that, they stop thinking logically and keep throwing good money after bad.

That's why you need to get a third party objective marketing expert involved as soon as possible so you don't get sucked into that.

Rob Gramer: Yeah, I definitely agree.

So let's say we've found a good market. We've found somebody, let's use the golf market because both you and I know that golfers will buy anything you put in front of them.

So let's say there's an inventor who has a golf invention. So he know the market, he's got the invention. Let's say it's a $50 product. What would kind of be your next step for that person right there?

Doberman Dan: First thing I do is, that the golf market is an easy one for me to research. A good thing about the market is that they are rabid.

You would be amazed at how much money a guy really into golf or girl really into golf will invest in their hobby.

So if we can prove that there is something that golf market wants you maybe on to something.

And it's easy to confirm that, you know I have access to lists of buyers in the golf markets and numerous markets.

So we can look up what golfers have been buying over the past several years and how they have been buying it, have they been buying it online, through

23

magazine ads, through direct mails, in retail stores, how often they have been buying, what price points they have been buying, give us a pretty detailed information about that and so again that will tell us if there really is a demand there.

Let's say your cost of manufacturing that, you figure out, is going to be, let's say $30. But the market will not pay more than $40 to $49 for that.

Well manufacturing, advertising cost and everything else, you know we can figure out that is not going to fly.

You either have got to get your manufacturing cost way lower or you just going to have ATP(abandon the project) and move on to something else.

Rob Gramer: That's interesting, what you just said is that you are trying to see in the marketplace what other people are buying and how much they are spending for something.

And then you are going to want to base your product roughly on the price that they're spending.

And the reason for this is because if John, Jack, Luke and Frank all spend

24

$60 on a golf product and you go introduce something that's fairly similar and you try to sell for $150, you already know ,it's going to be kinda hard to do.

They are not used to spending that much money on something that's similar, so you are going to already have an uphill battle.

Doberman Dan: Yeah, exactly. In many markets there are mental barriers established for pricing.

So, Rob, if you go to Barnes and Nobles today and you want to buy a book, I mean what are you going to pay for that book?

Rob Gramer: Let's say $15 to $30.

Doberman Dan: Okay, I mean that's pretty much the established price points for books.

So imagine Barnes and Nobles tells you every book in here is between $15 and $30 dollars but that book you want to buy today Rob, that is a $100.

Rob Gramer: No, forget about it.

Doberman Dan: Exactly. And that's the same in all other markets.

There are established price points for certain things.

There's ways to sell at higher prices but we don't have time to get into that.

When you are trying to prove the concept , you want to see what the average prices that people have been proven to pay for it or are paying for it now.

Rob Gramer: Basically what are you saying here is that somebody can use these strategies...let's say I want to go after the golf market.

Now I am going to research the golf market and I know the product is $50. They are willing to pay roughly about $50.

So now the person can basically backward engineer and say ok, I have got this idea. Now if I can produce it at 2 dollars and sell at 50 dollars, now we've got a pretty good chance of making some money there.

Doberman Dan: Yeah, exactly. I would find that very encouraging if all those criteria were met.

Rob Gramer: Got it, ok.

And you are actually right. This is way different than how most inventors operate. They wake up, they walk downstairs, they start making coffee and they break their coffee machine and say "oh, I can make a better version of this" and then they go make a better version and then, all of a sudden have a $5000 coffee machine.

But most people won't pay more than 200 bucks for one.

They are not going to spend $5000 on this coffee machine because the market is just not going to bare it.

Doberman Dan: That's right

Rob Gramer: We've gone through step one, we've gone through step two. We have a product that the market is going to bare, there is a market for it and they are going to buy it.

What would you advise our imaginary inventor to do next?

Doberman Dan: Well, do you want me to let the cat out of the bag and reveal like our big secret?

Rob Gramer: I want you to tell our listeners exactly what you would do if you had a gun to your head and if you had to make money tomorrow.

I want you to reveal everything in Dan's magic box

Doberman Dan: Ok, well, first of all I have to reveal some somewhat embarrassing stuff about myself.

In the past, I have treated projects like this and my entrepreneurial ventures more like gambling than business.

Not smart.

You know what, a few times it paid off bigger than I could've possibly imagined and what a thrill that was.

But most of the time it turned out really, really bad. So I am pretty conservative now until I get proof of concept.

In fact I am more conservative with my own projects, but I am almost like a miser when a client hires me.

I mean I picture myself as this big elephant and the first thing I am going to do...because now you are my client...you are under my protection, is give me your checkbook.

So I am this big elephant and I sit on that checkbook and they can't get at it.

Maybe this guy wants to sell you ad space in a magazine. Maybe you're thinking about advertising in the yellow pages. Maybe you want to plop a few hundred bucks in google ads.

Nope, you know my big fat butt is getting on your checkbook and I ain't moving.

So I am pretty conservative.

Here's what I do and what I recommend my clients do, before they go to all the time and energy and expense of having the product sourced and finding manufacturers and getting engineers involved or all these expensive CAD programs...

...and all that business that goes along with it, you know, who knows how many thousands, hundreds of thousands of dollars product development cost.

We don't even know, I mean we have a good idea that things going to fly but until we actually get somebody paying us for it, we don't know for sure.

So my secret is I go cheap and I recommend they create some sort of report, informational report or booklet about that topic that could be sold to that market.

I will give you an example.

Rob, you are working with somebody who is just getting into the supplement business, okay?

So they could, you know talk with a PHD or chemist about formulation, work on formulations then find what we call a private label laboratory, that's a laboratory that makes your products for you and puts your company label on it.

And you know, who knows how much initial quantity you have to order?

In some cases I have seen people have tens of thousands of dollars tied up in

30

a product before they even know if it's going to fly.

Let's say they want to formulate a product for joint health.

Before you get all that trouble, just write a report about it.

And see if you can sell that.

If you can sell that, well , then you can definitely sell a nutritional supplement product on joint health.

That's my big secret for testing as cheaply as possible and painlessly as possible.

Rob Gramer: Hmm, so what you are saying is that if I have an idea, I could spend say a quarter of million dollars hiring engineers, designers and all those source up to kind of go through the process of making it or…..let's say $50,000 to make it and then try to sell that to the market.

Or I can spend 2,3,4,5 days a week writing a report which will cost me a grand total of say $1, maybe $2 in pencil and paper. And then try to sell that report.

Go to www.inventionprep.com to learn how to start profiting off your idea in the next 30 days.

And if I go ahead and If I sell that report, if I am successful selling that, then it might make sense to go to the actual product.

Are you saying you want to not spend the $250,000 and you want to spend maybe $2 on the idea?

Doberman Dan: Yeah, you've summed it up perfectly.

That's exactly right.

I mean which one you would rather lose? $2 or $250,000?

I have done both. I can highly recommend you only loose $2.

Rob Gramer: And the funny thing is you mentioned supplements...

...so the client that I am working with, we had the idea roughly about 2 weeks ago, 3 weeks ago.

And we are going to go to the market next week!

And again we are doing this report style so we don't have a ton of money invested...my computer which I already had so that didn't cost anything...and it took us 3 weeks to put all together.

I have a friend of mine who came to me with another friend about a year and half ago for a supplement. I talked to her about two days ago and she just now got the formulation put together.

She ordered about 2000 bottles. So this past year and a half, she is going through getting investors, putting the product together and she has no idea if she will sell it or not.

So it's been year and a half and probably already spent about thirty to forty thousand dollars of either her money or various investor's money before she even knows the thing is going to sell or not, work or not.

Doberman Dan: Yeah, we sure want to stop people from doing that.

You know, a contributing to factor to that is also, (I should probably issue a warning here) a lot of advertising reps are all just sales people.

They just sell you advertising but yet they position themselves as marketing experts.

Say the ad or the magazine you want to test an ad in or a website you want to test running a banner ad on or you are going to speak with an ad representative. A lot of time they try to position themselves as marketing experts.

They are not.

They are just sales people and they are trying to sell you an ad.

So a lot of people get bad advice thinking that they are getting marketing advice from marketing expert and they spend way too much money on advertising.

This is the trick they always play. I love this and I love shooting this down because I have got 20 years of real hard numbers and facts, proof, this is not true.

But this is a trick that media reps, the advertising reps say ...you need to run your ad multiple times because people need to see it more than once for it to work.

So just running your add once isn't good. We need to gets you in what they call an insert order, in other words an order for 3 months, 6 months. We need to get you in there for twelve issues, twelve months...

...and it's complete BS.

20 years of experience in this, if the ad doesn't work one time, it won't work multiple times. In fact if it works one time, response always goes down with multiple insertions.

So be careful who you take advice from.

Rob Gramer: the people reading the magazine have already seen it so they are not going to respond again if they respond the first time.

Doberman Dan: Exactly

Rob Gramer: Yes and you bring up a very important point.

And it's something people rarely hear.

These people...be it patent attorneys, marketing professionals, people who are selling ad space for magazines, engineers, designers, web designers, graphic designers, any of these people, they are running their own business.

Their job first and foremost is to get you to hire them so they can do whatever is that they do.

So whenever you sit down with these people, off course, they are going to

35

tell you, off course the engineers going to tell you, oh yeah we need 15 different designs, off course the website guys going to say, oh yeah, you have to have this fancy 15 page website with an about me page, a contact us, a blog and all sorts of stuff.

And most times it's bullshit...

We've both seen where we can put together a webpage, a simple one page webpage, and a link to the report with a paypal button.

You don't even have to pay for that, you just sign up with paypal and then you buy some traffic in the market that you are looking at and then you sell it right from that. And putting that together doesn't take very long at all.

Really, if I have somebody put a gun to my head and I had an idea I wanted to see if I could monetize it or not, I should be able to get all the information I need on whether or not this is a good project inside of 30 days.

Any inventor who has spent more than 30 days and they don't know whether or not they are making any money from their idea, well, I am sorry to say but you are probably spending more money and more time than you need to on this.

Doberman Dan: That's exactly right, Yeah.

Rob Gramer: So Dan , now that we have the product and you've got the market, is it just a case of now putting together an ad and putting in front of people to see what happens? Is that the next step or is there something else involved there?

Doberman Dan: Yes that would be eventually the next step, I mean, there's still little more market research to do.

Each different market or sub niche of market, is like its own little culture and there's things you need to do to figure out.

If you are not one of them so to speak...

Like my first mail order business was in the body building market. Now I was one of them. I knew the culture and knew the lingo.

But if it's something that you are not one of them, you need to learn that culture, how they think, the mindset and the lingo.

Rob, you and I looked at a website just yesterday for a guy who sold something to computer engineers. So you probably understood it more than me but me looking at it, the lingo that they used on their website was like Greek.

So you need to find all that stuff out.

You need to find out how people in your market talk, the jargon they use.

So that's all part of the market research, once that's understood it's a matter of, I would like to say running it up to flag pole and see how many people salute it.

Which to me means getting it out there in the market through whichever media we are going to use...either online media or offline media like a magazine ad, direct mail stuff like that. And what I mean by people saluting it, I am talking about saluting with their wallet, with their credit card.

They actually cough up money and buy it.

Go to www.inventionprep.com to learn how to start profiting off your idea in the next 30 days.

Rob Gramer: Hmm, so I think that's a very important point because a lot of the inventors that I have talked to, they seem to think that they need to get the thing packaged in a box on a store shelf or they need to take out T.V advertisement or something along those lines.

Whereas what you are saying here is that no, that's not the case. You can go direct to the consumer, talk directly to the person that is as going to ultimately pay for your product and then convince them to buy it.

And this can be done very cheaply for hundreds of dollars inside of 30 days rather than hundreds of thousands of dollars spending over a couple of years.

Doberman Dan: Absolutely, something else I have done, it's not as reliable.

Really what I really want to see, I want to see that people in the market are going to part with money for this product but I have also done the report deal that I was telling about.

Go to www.inventionprep.com to learn how to start profiting off your idea in the next 30 days.

Had a report created and offered it free in exchange for someone giving me their email address.

If I was testing something online, I put up a website with a short description of the report and a call to action as just simply enter your email to get this free report on whatever the topic is.

And you can still you know, maybe get, you can get a feel for the market that way because I still would like I say rather see a bunch of people wanting to buy it.

But if you do that and you can't get people to take it for free, well then there's no way you are going to sell it.

Rob Gramer: And just so everybody listening understands, you don't want to tell the public about it, because obviously you don't want somebody stealing your idea.

But what we are talking about right now ...we are not really revealing what the invention is.

And there's a lot more that goes into this but realize that you can test your ideas to the marketplace without actually revealing what the invention is.

There's a lot of strategy that goes into this, there's different ways to go about doing this but realize that this strategy that we are talking about here doesn't necessarily involve you telling people what your idea is either.

Doberman Dan: Yeah ,exactly. I am glad that you pointed it out.

Rob Gramer: So you gave a lot of great information. Is there anything else that you would like to hit upon before we call this interview a wrap?

Doberman Dan: Not that I can think of. I think we have covered the most important points and hopefully any inventor or potential inventor listening to this has picked up on the fact that we want to save them from all the mistakes in lost time and lost money that many inventors are falling prey to.

And just let them know that there's a tested and proven process for determining if their invention is a good idea.

Whether or not they should go forward and it doesn't have to be time consuming or expensive at all.

Rob Gramer: Yeah, and just so everybody listening to knows that you can access all this for free, we've got these all laid out on our website.

It's www.inventionprep.com. If you go there, you can put your name and email in, there's no cost and you can get all the information on how to do this, all laid out for you.

Doberman Dan: Absolutely.

Rob gramer: Thanks Dan, thanks for the call.

Doberman Dan: My Pleasure

Want more Doberman Dan? Visit his website at www.dobermandan.com. He has tons of free cool stuff waiting for you there.

Is There a Market for Your Idea?

Who is going to buy your idea? What are they willing to pay for it? What media (TV, radio, mail, online, retail) do they like to buy?

These are the questions you must answer if you have any hope of turning your ideas into cash.

The difficult (and time consuming part) is NOT creating a product...it's, digging up the information on your target market.

That's where I come in. I help people who have ideas and inventions (just like you) find out if there is a market big enough for your idea.

And if you're not ready to reveal your idea just yet...or...if you are already past this stage, I can also show you:

- How to save thousands of dollars on legal fees while patenting your invention
- How to find designers and engineers to create your ideas on paper and in real life (from sketches to prototypes, to mass manufacturing) quicker than you ever dreamed possible
- And, how to get all the money you need WITHOUT investors...usually within 30 days (AND you get to keep ALL your equity)

43

Go to www.inventionprep.com to learn how to start profiting off your idea in the next 30 days.

Most people think it takes a major investment of time and money to get their ideas off the ground.

Now you can start profiting from your ideas and inventions in as little as 30 days.

If you'd like me to help, just send an email to Rob@inventionprep.com and we'll take it from there.

Go to www.inventionprep.com to learn how to start profiting off your idea in the next 30 days.

Awesome Free Bonuses!

Visit www.inventionprep.com for free instant access to more free cool stuff like...

- Personal feedback from licensed patent professionals, engineers, and experienced marketers on how to protect, create, and sell your idea.
- How to save thousands on legal fees to protect your idea
- Quickly and cheaply create prototypes and final products (in days instead of weeks or months)
- Profit from your idea as quick as humanely possible...usually inside 30 days

Just go to www.inventionprep.com for instant access.

Go to www.inventionprep.com to learn how to start profiting off your idea in the next 30 days.

www.ingramcontent.com/pod-product-compliance
Lightning Source LLC
Chambersburg PA
CBHW071545170526
45166CB00004B/1564